The War, the Lift and the Separatists

A Play

By Novid Shaid

ISBN 978-0993044878

DEDICATION

To Britain, its people and to hope in troubled times

ACKNOWLEDGEMENTS

I would like to thank brother Masud Ahmed Khan, webmaster of **www.masud.co.uk** for kindly editing this play and for making pertinent and helpful suggestions.

INFORMATION ABOUT THE PLAY

This play contains twelve scenes.
The character of the woman is inspired by Valerie Solanas's tract, SCUM Manifesto, published in 1967.

NOTES ON NAMES, TERMS AND PRHASES

Asia- this name is pronounced like ass-e-a, with a strong, throaty initial 'a' phoneme. This is the Arabic name for the wife of Pharaoh in the Quran.

Chris Poyy- anagram for hypocrisy.

Hijra- 'making hijra"- refers to moving to a place for the sake of one's faith.

Jallabiyya- traditional, long tunic that Arabs wear culturally; lovely and comfortable to wear but some can use it as an afront to Western clothing.

Kafir/Kuffar/Kufs- unbeliever/unbelievers/slang for kafir. These words can be used derogatorily by extremists to otherize non-Muslims.

La Hawla Wa La Quwwata Illa Billa- prayer from the Quran: there is no power or strength except from Allah- this prayer is sometimes expressed as a sign of exasperation.

Mushtaq Takfir / Rehmat Fakir / Riza Annafs- these are satirical names, lampooning the extremist mindset. Mushtaq Takfir literally means-lover of excommunicating; Rehmat Fakir- impoverished of mercy; Riza Annafs- the narcissistic one.

Rossperg- anagram for Progress.

Roman Fattansis- anagram for Roman Fantasist.

Sabr- (Arabic) patience.

EPIGRAPH

The elevator algorithm, a simple algorithm by which a single elevator can decide where to stop, is summarized as follows:

Continue travelling in the same direction while there are remaining requests in that same direction.

If there are no further requests in that direction, then stop and become idle, or change direction if there are requests in the opposite direction.

The Day on which the secret things are rendered public

The Quran, 86:9

CHARACTER LIST- IN ORDER OF APPEARANCE

THE LIFT

THE MUSLIM

THE WOMAN

THE WHITE MAN

NEWS ANCHOR WOMAN

SHOPPING CENTRE MANAGER

VOICE OF FIREBRAND PREACHER

ASIA

GRAMPS

HOPE

VOICE OF THE NEWSCASTER

ROMAN FATTANSIS'S VOICE

MUSHTAQ TAKFIR'S VOICE

AMERICAN'S VOICE

SHOP ASSISTANT'S VOICE

SECURITY GUARD'S VOICE

CUSTOMER'S VOICE

MEMBER OF PUBLIC'S VOICE

CHARLIE'S VOICE

ASSISTANT MANAGER

ENGINEER'S VOICE

NEWS ANCHOR MAN

SCENE ONE

(We hear the whine and the crash of a lift grinding to a halt. The stage reveals a lift in a shopping centre car park containing three outlandish people: a Muslim fanatic, a white racist man and an ultra-feminist woman. They stand apart, in shock and in anticipation.

Suddenly the lift's phone starts buzzing, the woman involuntarily moves and presses the speaker button. The unearthly and distant voice of the lift speaks)

VOICE OF THE LIFT:

I am Lift, request your direction.

(The characters are dumbfounded and remain standing. We hear the ominous stretching and flexing of the lift's cords. Lights fade.)

SCENE TWO

(An anchorwoman for a Newscast appears and announces the day's top stories. In the background, there could be relevant music, images and graphics that accompany the newscast.)

ANCHOR WOMAN:

Good afternoon and today's top stories. Separatist Militias gain victories and territories, as the ongoing conflict in the central state of Rossperg threatens to spill over into neighbouring states. These developments come as further damaging blows to the Rosspergan authorities, after the recent leakages of classified recordings of their ministers sanctioning torture and 'de-radicalisation' programmes for captured militants. Our Foreign Office is keeping close attention to the unfolding events in Rossperg which have already resulted in the displacement of thousands of people from the troubled region. The separatist militants have been calling for an autonomous state after what they feel has been years of oppression and suppression under Rosspergan state control. Comments from the Rosspergan Foreign Minister, Roman Fattansis and Foreign Office Minister Chris Poyy to come later.

The trial of three would-be terrorists is beginning today. The three men, Mushtaq Takfir, Rehmat Faqir and Jabran Kabir are charged with conspiring to blow-up various landmarks as well as plotting the beheading of the Muslim politician, Riza Annafs. The trial begins today at the Old Bailey and we will be following developments there.

GB Telecom has received more complaints about the broadcasting of private telephone conversations onto medium wave radio programmes. Members of the public have been shocked to find extracts of their conversations interrupting radio programmes, some of which have been broadcasted to thousands of regular listeners. GB Telecom is still perplexed about the situation and are still unable to locate the exact problems, but are working closely with the broadcasting authority to resolve the situation.

(Smiling.) And finally, in our special item, the mystifying reports of the new 'awakening' phenomenon continue to grow as a Christian man from the Bible belt in the US believes he has captured, on digital video, his 'toaster' communicating and exhorting him to prepare for Armageddon. *(Her introduction ends with news music, EXIT- lights fade.)*

SCENE THREE

(The stage reveals the appearance of the first scene: a representation of a lift in a shopping centre car park, open at the front, so the audience can see the action that takes place inside.

In the background, nauseating shopping centre music can be heard, which carries on in the lift.

A Muslim, a young Asian, appears in Arab garb and enters the lift. He wears a grey jallabiyya and black skull cap, with a healthy beard reaching his neck, and has this intense seriousness about him. Moments pass as he presses the button and the lift pronounces "Level 5 Going Down", when suddenly two more people dash into the lift just before it shuts. A white man in his twenties, skin-head, tight jeans, trainers, bomber jacket, cropped hair. After gathering himself, he regards the Muslim next to him with a savage look. The Muslim, in turn is frowning at the back of next person who is a woman. She is also white and has a short bob of hair which is pulled back with a hair band reaching her ears, wears her t-shirt over jeans. She is glancing at both men momentarily, giving a haughty, sarcastic stare every now and then. They are all extremely striking in their appearance.

They now stand in a triangular formation to ensure separation: the Muslim at the front so he can leave first, the white man behind him to the left, and the woman to the right.

They remain silent as the lift begins to the travel, except that the white man now regards the woman with contempt and the woman stares at the Muslim's dress up and down with an unsympathetic look.

Suddenly, the lift begins to tremble before it reaches level 4. The customers grip each side of the lift and hold on, then in a flash, the lift grinds to a halt, throwing each of the travellers to the ground. They end up in a mixed pile on the floor, almost entangled: the white man on the Muslim and the woman grasping onto the white man. The lights fizzle on and off until they sustain their power once again. The lift stops shaking.

There is silence for a while as the people lie there entangled.

They slowly come to their senses, the Muslim cries things like "Let me up", "You're choking me", *The white man cries,* "I can't, she's on me!" *And the woman finally gets up and three retreat to each side of the lift, standing awkwardly, brushing themselves down. Then they kind of occupy their territory, disturbed.)*

MUSLIM:

(replacing his cap carefully.) Right, we better phone the emergency line; it's normally by the buttons *(he speaks English fluently without an immigrant accent which surprises the others.)*

WHITE MAN:

(who is next to the buttons, looks suspiciously at the Muslim then he presses the telephone/speaker button and finally receives a "Hello".) Hello, the bloody lift's broken down, we're stuck between the fifth and fourth level. What you gonna do about that mate?

SHOPPING CENTRE MANAGER'S VOICE:

(his matter-of-fact voice can be heard through the speakers.) Hello, this is John Davis shopping centre manager, you're through to the emergency line, first of all is anyone hurt?

WHITE MAN:

(He looks to the others who confirm with a nod that they are ok.)
No, we're all fine. A little shaken but we'll live.

SHOPPING CENTRE MANAGER'S VOICE:

That's wonderful, well then, I would like to express my apologies for this inconvenience. We will have you out as soon as possible, so please remain calm. I've had a look at the system and you're not in any danger, *(The listeners look at each other in disbelief.)* it appears as if the lift has stopped and is not moving.

WHITE MAN:

Well, blow me down! I would never have thought of that.

SHOPPING CENTRE MANAGER'S VOICE:

Ahem, ahem, yes quite, don't mean to state the obvious but the fact is the programming of the lift for requests going up and down has failed, and it is locked in the command to remain idle. We will have to get some emergency engineers to get it working again, in fact, we have already called them and we are expecting them to arrive very soon. This hasn't happened before, but I do expect the lift to be working with in an hour.

ALL THREE:

An hour!

SHOPPING CENTRE MANAGER'S VOICE:

Or less, I hope. Er, how many of you are there?

WHITE MAN:

There's three of us, two blokes and, er... A woman.

SHOPPING CENTRE MANAGER'S VOICE:

Does anyone there suffer from claustrophobia, or asthma?

WHITE MAN:

Well I don't. You heard the guy, *(To the Muslim, slowly and patronisingly.)* do you suffer from a fear of being enclosed? Do you understand what I'm saying mate?

MUSLIM:

(Firmly, annoyed.) Yeh, I understood him completely, I don't suffer from claustrophobia or xenophobia so I should be alright. *(The white man narrows his eyes in response.)*

WOMAN:

No, I'm fine with that.

WHITE MAN

(On the phone.) No, we're alright with that, but it might get quite stuffy in here and we'll have trouble breathing after a while.

SHOPPING CENTRE MANAGER'S VOICE:

Well, as I said, we should have you out soon, the accident hasn't disturbed the air-circulation. I would advise you to remain seated to conserve your energy and to economise your breathing. I'll keep you regularly informed on what's going on. If you have any problems, please don't hesitate to alert me between then by pressing the speaker button with which you can hear me and I can hear you.

(The White Man presses the button to switch-off the phone.)

(They remain still, looking at each other awkwardly.)

(The White Man breaks the silence.)

WHITE MAN:

Well bloody hell! I thought that was some sort of terrorist attack. Especially as Bin Laden here is among us.

MUSLIM:

Excuse me?

WHITE MAN:

(Who doesn't directly talk to either the Muslim or the woman but with an air of thinking aloud.) Did you hear him? He knew exactly where the phone was, sounds like he's been studying his lifts *(He is cut off.)*

MUSLIM:

(Intimidatingly.) You don't need to be a terrorist to work out that every lift has an emergency phone, only a bloody idiot like you wouldn't have the brains for that. And what a prat you are, we're in an emergency situation here and you're making frankly racist comments to my face.

(The woman remains withdrawn but the growing anger of the men is unsettling her.)

MUSLIM:

And I tell you what, you make a comment like that again and I'll beat the crap out of you here and now, do you understand *(Moving closer to the white man.)*

WHITE MAN:

(Growing in rage.) You trying threaten me mate!?

MUSLIM:

I'm not trying mate, I'm giving you a guarantee.

WHITE MAN:

Well then let's see you carry out that guarantee you stupid Paki!!
(He shoves the Muslim hard on the chest.)

MUSLIM:

White trash!

(The Muslim grabs the White man by the neck and thrusts him against the lift, suddenly the woman screams. At this moment, the lift begins to shudder dangerously as they begin their assaults.)

WOMAN:

Stop it you idiots, you could kill us all!

(The two stop and remember the precarious situation they are in and stop fighting. The lift calms down. The men retreat to opposite ends of the lift, like boxers in-between rounds.)

WOMAN:

Typical men! Always trying to prove themselves and show their power, pathetic!

WHITE MAN:

And who the bloody hell are you, the leader of the lesi party, mind your own business.

MUSLIM:

Oi! you watch the way you speak to women.

WOMAN:

You don't have to speak up for me Abdul, I can speak for myself, I'm not a concubine from your harem.

MUSLIM:

Well pardon me for being polite, typical lesbian!

WOMAN:

Well, I am damned surprise that you actually know what we're called. I thought there wasn't a term for us in your vocabulary, like you don't want us to exist.

MUSLIM:

Oh, we have a term for you alright, unnatural.

WOMAN:

Right, Mr Believer's gonna give us a lecture about the balance in nature and Allah created us from clay, male and female, two by two.

MUSLIM:

Oh, and I'm really surprised that you actually remembered that it takes a male and female to create another life.

WHITE MAN:

Weah! Bin Laden actually has a point there, Miss Greer. I mean no offence, but do you have to broadcast to the rest of the world that you like a bit of your own sort, if you get what I mean? In any case, I'm sure there's a man out there waiting for you... Somewhere! *(He laughs)*

WOMAN:

Well, this is just my luck, I'm stuck in a lift with two of the biggest scumbags in the world: a Muslim fanatic and a white chauvinist dog!!!

MUSLIM:

Look, I tried to stick up for you and all you could say was that I was trying to make you my second wife.

WHITE MAN:

Go Usama, get in there my son, are you allowed to marry them?

WOMAN:

Shut-up you low-life disgrace to the human race! *(Whispering.)* Oh, give me strength!

(The Muslim takes a great sigh, obviously wound up. They are silent for a while. The white man stares at the Muslim who is now mouthing some sort of prayer.)

WOMAN:

Oh, would you bloody mind keeping your prayers to yourself, all these people know is prayer.

WHITE MAN:

Yep, and opening corner shops.

MUSLIM:

You're both just a pair of white trash, right, and if you don't keep your filthy comments to yourself, you'll regret it, and I couldn't care less what happens to the lift.

(The Muslim retreats and doesn't say a word. The other two fail to respond. There is a long silence.)

fade off the other two and focus on the Muslim who
as if to himself.)

MUSLIM:

Just a few more days and I'll be far away from your kafir ways.
(Lights fade.)

SCENE FOUR

(The lights now focus on the Muslim man's house and sitting room. The Muslim sits on a leather chair next to a coffee table checking through travel documents and passports. His house is well-presented and he is an affluent computer programmer. He lives with his wife, Asia and they have been married for four years. They met and fell in love when they were younger and became more religious and strict after marriage. The Muslim has gone further to the point that his religious sentiments are extremist and divisive. Asia, his wife, has a more reasonable and perceptive approach.

The main focus of the room is the fireplace. Above it is draped a gigantic black flag of the Islamic Kalima (article of faith). The TV is audible echoing a hate speech video by an unidentified firebrand British Muslim preacher. His subject is the inferiority of the unbelievers and the necessity of emigration to another Muslim country to escape the filth of the West. The Muslim looks up every now and then, assenting to what he hears, but the impression is that he has played this tape many times.)

(He continues checking through his documents.)

VOICE OF FIREBRAND PREACHER ON THE TV:

Yes, my brothers! They don't just want you to follow their rules, they want you to adopt their filthy culture as well. A culture of women presenting themselves as cattle waiting to be mounted by bullish, yobbish men in night clubs, whilst exposing their nakedness and filth. Very soon they'll be at it in the streets my brothers. They have no shame. Can you imagine bringing up your children in this place, surrounded by this filth? Do you want your children living within the muck of their teenage pregnancies, binge drinking, one-night stands, talents shows, pornography and shameless consumerism? These kuffar who are not worth one hair in the nostril of a believer! Who are not worth the very cattle that graze in their fields, the very cattle that they themselves behave like!

And that's why it's a duty upon us to distance ourselves from these people my brothers..

MUSLIM:

(Looking at the door, lessening the volume on the TV.) Asia! What's happening?

ASIA:

(Her voice is heard.) It's just coming! Have a bit of sabr!

MUSLIM:

(With annoyance.) Ashi! I'm starved! I haven't eaten all day!

(Asia enters, carrying a tray full of cooked food. She wears a hijab and black jallabiya. She is the epitome of patience and strength.)

ASIA:

(Coming in.) Alright, alright, I'm sorry, it took longer than expected, that's all.

MUSLIM:

I'm not having a go, but I haven't eaten since last night, I didn't even have breakfast. I've been so busy sorting everything out for the move. Passports, tickets, subletting forms, the list is endless, la hawla wa la quwatta illa billah!

ASIA:

Well, tuck into this now before it gets cold.

MUSLIM:

Okay, calm down let me just finish off here!

(Asia's face clouds over in annoyance then she composes herself swiftly.)

MUSLIM:

(Noticing her hijab.) How come you're still wearing your hijab?

ASIA:

I told you I'm going to my sister's after dinner and I've already put it in place, weren't you listening. Ya Allah, give me strength.

MUSLIM:

Okay! Alright! *(Whining.)* I was only asking! *(Pause.)* I do like to feast my eyes on you my love, that's all.

ASIA:

Oh, thank you *(She smiles, with a hint of sarcasm.)*

(Pause.)

ASIA:

(Begins eating and makes a discreet prayer before starting then she notices the talk.) When are you going to stop listening to this stuff? He is just so negative! If he hates these people so much then why doesn't he live somewhere else, honestly! Don't you get bored of listening to the same talk every day?

MUSLIM:

(Still checking his documents and ignoring the food.) No, never. Every time I hear him, I pick up something new. The more I listen to what he has to say, the more it makes sense.

ASIA:

(Reasonably.) Yes, but can't you play something else for a change? I mean, honestly, I know we both agreed on cutting down on regular TV, but listening to this guy everyday is excessive. What about all those videos you got on Islamic history and those Nature programmes. *(She notices his food.)* Your food is getting cold.

MUSLIM:

(Notices his food.) Oh yes, sorry. *(He puts the documents aside; the video carries on; he takes a few bites.)* Asia, you make the best curry in the whole world!!

(She smiles satisfyingly. He chews for a while, the speech has now become inaudible. The couple sit silently for a while.)

MUSLIM:

Yes, as I was saying, this man isn't afraid of telling the truth. He says it like it is- stuff the political correctness and fussing around- these kafirs will never be happy until we become one of them.

ASIA:

Oh really *(Bored.)*

MUSLIM:

And, in fact, even if we became like them, they still wouldn't accept us because we're Muslim. So that's why what this guy is saying is totally right- the more we live with these people, the more we become infected with what they have.

ASIA:

The only thing I'm infected by is your constant moaning and groaning. Haven't you got a good thing to say about people? I thought a good Muslim is supposed to be a mercy to the whole world. I don't see much mercy in your attitude.

MUSLIM:

There you go again Asia-sounding like the apologetics. I know you're not really like them sell-outs so I won't respond to your wind ups. But when we're gone- I'm gonna be happy to be away from these pathetic people who think they're Muslim and go on about stupidity like we have to live with kafirs in harmony and basically submit to their ways. That's kufr advice if I've ever heard it.

ASIA:

I don't know about submitting to anybody and or anything except Allah. But living in harmony sounds like common-sense to me.

MUSLIM:

Ah, ah Asia, playing with me again, I know what you're up to. You just want me to get wound up so I'll do the dishes but it won't work. Why would you want to live with a people who don't even know how to wash themselves? Honestly, I was just thinking about those ponces in the government. I bet none of them actually clean themselves after going to the loo. Can you imagine that? We're being led by people who don't even know how to wash themselves after using a bathroom. And that's just the way it is. *(Asia continues to eat, listening half-interested, half-daydreaming.)* Did I tell you about my boss. Oh my God! He earns more than 100k a year, he's in charge of millions of pounds and hundreds of staff- but the man is one dirty kuff. I was in the loo during a lunch break doing my wudu. When in comes the boss, Richard. And guess what? He didn't even wash his hands when he'd finished. He came up to the mirror, stroked his moustache, asked me how I was doing and told me how much of an asset I was to the company, patted himself down and then he just walked out. I mean what a dirty man- and people like him are our bosses. No wonder things are going crazy in this country, impure kufs at the top with urine hands. *(Asia drops her food momentarily.)* Oh sorry.

ASIA:

At least I won't hear your complaints when we reach Riyadh. What's the itinerary then?

MUSLIM:

Yes, the itinerary. Basically, we'll do the umrah first and stay in Mecca for five nights, then we go immediately to Riyadh to our- and wait for it- our five-star luxury flat in a special Islamic area, no kuffs allowed, it's only Arabs who live there.

ASIA:

(Absorbing her new home.) 5-star accommodation, wow! Remind me, what are we talking about?

MUSLIM:

We're talking about these massive apartments, three bedrooms, two lounges, state of the art kitchen and bathroom, parking place, clean area, shopping centres not too far away, but then there's also the Islamic environment, women dressed accordingly, mosques everywhere, and the best bit, absolutely no KUFFAR!

ASIA:

I like the sound of the apartment, and we've got my relatives who also live in Riyadh remember. I'll miss mum and my sisters though.

MUSLIM:

I'll miss them too and my own parents, but they can visit us there if they want. *(More intimate.)* We'll be much better off there. It will be our hijra away from this godforsaken place of a country where you're treated like a third-class citizen despite the fact that you're making 60 grand a year. Away from this hell-hole of people living without meaning, without a reason for their existence, with all these slags, sluts, beer bellies, with gays getting married, single-parent families, and people just wasting their lives away while imposing their kafir ways on the rest of us and the rest of the world. I don't want to bring my future children up in this place. *(Asia smiles sarcastically.)* And I tell you what, if this Rossperg crisis continues, we'll be in the safest place, because if war comes here, you'll see these people for what they really are. All suits and professionals on the outside, but animals on the inside. Good job we're leaving when we are.

ASIA:

Oh and that reminds me. I heard our kind, non-Muslim neighbours had recently donated £1000 pound to our mosque.

MUSLIM:

Ha, ha, very funny. *(Finishing his meal.)* Well, I need to gather some last minute stuff from up town, get a few more passport size photographs and a digital camera and I'll be back soon. Imagine it Asia, in two days we'll be away for good!!! *(Lights Fade.)*

SCENE FIVE

(Lights reveal and resume the situation in the lift. The three individuals sit silently at each end of the lift. The cheap muzak carries on, indicating that the speakers are still working despite the malfunctions. Silence. The individuals each check their mobile phones intermittently but find there is no reception in the lift, and strangely their mobiles will not even turn on.)

WHITE MAN:

Is your phone working?

(Neither the Muslim or the woman answers.)

WHITE MAN:

Look, I'm just asking a simple question, you don't have to be so frigging uptight about it!

MUSLIM:

No, mine's not working.

WOMAN:

Mine neither.

WHITE MAN:

Very strange! I fully charged mine this morning.

MUSLIM:

Same here. I can't think why they won't turn on. We won't get any reception in here, but the phones should come on.

WOMAN:

My phone has never done this before.

WHITE MAN:

Hang about. *(Pointing to the ceiling.)* They've got a bloody CCTV camera in here! And he was trying to put on that he couldn't see us before!

WOMAN:

Yes, they can witness the wonderful time we're having.

WHITE MAN:

(Still looking up at the camera.) Well, don't get any ideas mate *(To the Muslim, pretending to blow himself up.)* Or it will be caught on candid camera!! *(Laughs at his own humour.)*

WOMAN:

(Not amused.) Look, don't start please, we don't want another argument in this lift.

MUSLIM:

It's alright. I'm not offended that easily.

WHITE MAN:

(Incredulously.) Not offended too easily... Have you read any Salman Rushdie recently?

MUSLIM:

Right that's enough *(Stands up menacingly.)*

WOMAN:

Look will you just cut it out please, we can't afford to have a fight in this lift!

(Just before the Muslim has a chance for retaliation, suddenly the phone starts buzzing. The Muslim presses the speaker button and is clearly frustrated).

SHOPPING CENTRE MANAGER'S VOICE:

Hello people, how's are you doing?

MUSLIM:

How are we doing? What do you mean? Can't you see and hear what's going on. This poor excuse for a human is subjecting me to racist abuse and I'm this close to sorting it out my own way, right here, right now.

WOMAN:

I am afraid to say it's true. This man here is out of order.

WHITE MAN:

What a load of bollocks!

WOMAN:

These two already had a scuffle and now he's made another comment. I am feeling very uncomfortable in here, can't you hurry up with the lift.

SHOPPING CENTRE MANAGER'S VOICE:

Madam, I assure you that we are working as fast as we can, and I am confident that the time frame I have given you will suffice for the lift to be in working order again.

WOMAN:

What about the situation between these two?

SHOPPING CENTRE MANAGER'S VOICE:

What about it?

WOMAN:

We could end up with a fight in here.

WHITE MAN:

Look, look. There's not going to be a fight. I haven't made any comments. I've just been trying to lighten up the atmosphere.

SHOPPING CENTRE MANAGER'S VOICE:

Well sir whatever you're doing, it seems to be unsettling the woman so please be patient while we get the lift fixed.

WHITE MAN:

Okay, I will keep schtum from now on. I don't want any trouble.

MUSLIM:

Probably the best thing you've said so far pal.

SHOPPING CENTRE MANAGER'S VOICE:

(Pause.) Now, I must say, having just realised what you've said, I am becoming rather confused.

WHITE MAN:

Oh yeh, about what?

SHOPPING CENTRE MANAGER'S VOICE:

Well, I've been in my office with the CCTV watching your progress and... I don't understand.

WOMAN:

What's the problem?

SHOPPING CENTRE MANAGER'S VOICE:

Well, I've been watching you for the last quarter of an hour, and you were all just sitting there...quietly.

MUSLIM:

Yes, we were sitting here, but didn't you see or hear this guy abuse me?

SHOPPING CENTRE MANAGER'S VOICE:

That's the point. I have been watching you, and I can hear what you're saying as well, it's just a precaution, this isn't big brother or anything, but I have just watched you lot sit there quietly staring into space.

WOMAN:

There must be something wrong with your CCTV then, because it's been mayhem in here.

WHITE MAN:

And, on that note, none of our phones are working.

SHOPPING CENTRE MANAGER'S VOICE:

Yes, I'm sorry, but the lifts do disrupt the signals. There is no reception in the lifts unfortunately.

WHITE MAN:

No, I mean my phone doesn't even come on. Their phones don't work either. That can't just be a coincidence.

SHOPPING CENTRE MANAGER'S VOICE:

Strange. I will ask the engineers on that and get back to you. Anyway, I'll keep you informed about the progress and I will get back to you within the next quarter of an hour.

ALL:

Thanks.

WHITE MAN:

What the bloody hell is going on here?

WOMAN:

Either this shopping centre is fully malfunctioning or Friday the 13th must have come early.

(They sit silently.)

WHITE MAN:

I don't like the bloody sound of this one bit. I had things to do today and instead I'm stuck here in a pissing lift with... *(The lights fades off the Muslim and the woman and the white man quietly says to himself.)* Anyway, I'll be clear of the lot of them soon, the queers, the Pakis, the wogs, the lot of them. *(Lights fade.)*

SCENE SIX

(The lights reveal the white man's sitting room which is in a typical council-style flat. A British Flag is draped over the mantle- piece. Once again, two sofas face the audience and a TV. The white man also sits watching, close to travel documents on a coffee table. He is dressed in his t-shirts and jeans, listening intently to a news broadcast about the group of young Muslims who were mentioned earlier and were caught in the process of planning a terrorist attack.

The white man is unemployed and lives with his grand dad, his mother's dad. The white man is fairly young but has developed a deeply entrenched bitterness to all foreigners and foreignness in Britain. He is passionately nationalistic and xenophobic.)

VOICE OF NEWSCAST:

The jury have been hearing recordings of telephone conversations between Mushtaq Takfir and his accomplices, Rehmat Faqir and Jabran Kabir. Their conversations include their organisation of meeting points and reconnaissance to the targeted landmarks. The jury will also watch the captured suicide speeches on their laptops.

WHITE MAN:

Gramps!!!

GRAMPS:

On my way son, on my way! *(From off-stage.)*

WHITE MAN

How long does it take it make a simple cup of tea mate! You haven't gone all arthritic on me because that would make you one alf a right arse! *(Laughs at his own joke.)*

GRAMPS:

(Entering with tea and biscuits on a tray.) Don't be cheeky son, I'm still young and energetic enough to give you a right arse whipping.

WHITE MAN:

Orr, cheers gramps.

GRAMPS:

So what's the progress?

WHITE MAN:

(Listing each item.) Passports- check, tickets- check, travellers' cheques- check, *(He smiles.)* and here are the keys to our, sorry gramps, to your dream, stupendous, monstrous retirement home where me and you will hold nude barbecues with all the finest Ozzie women in the area!!!

GRAMPS:

Core blimey, you ain't half looking forward to it.

WHITE MAN:

Gramps, I'm so itching to go that I can hardly sleep, I really feel this is gonna get me back into shape.

GRAMPS:

And hopefully get a job at the same time.

WHITE MAN:

As I said gramps, I'm gonna give it 100% in the Oz, I just know that away from this place, I'll be able to think more clearly because I'll be around my own kind, unlike here where you're surrounded by every kind of illegal alien breed in the book.

GRAMPS:

Yes, hopefully you'll get some work, and I'll just sit back and enjoy the ride as they say.

WHITE MAN:

I'll enjoy the ride as well- the sand, sea and surf kind of ride! *(Gestures the hourglass shape of beach babes.)*

GRAMPS:

I told you boy, your focus is work-that was the deal- don't let me down now.

WHITE MAN:

Oh, sure gramps, and once I get a job, I'll be paying my way, chipping in, giving my share, don't you worry.

GRAMPS:

Now doesn't that sound familiar... I remember you when you were in your nappies, your poor mum had passed away, and you were as happy-go-lucky then as you are now, it's freaky.

WHITE MAN:

Look gramps, now I don't wanna go into one again, but you can't not be happy-go-lucky here because all the opportunities are snatched away from yer by the curry squad, the Poles, the Romanians, the Hungarians, hungry, scrounging asylum seekers from bloody Africa and the Arabs, and the rest of the universe who've decided to pitch up tent in our green and pleasant land.

GRAMPS:

Look, let's just enjoy our tea, I didn't mean to get you uptight, what's on the box?

WHITE MAN:

(Not listening.) Gramps, we're losing the battle here, why don't you understand. A white man just doesn't have the power he used to have before. We're not treated in the way we're supposed to be. Sell-outs in the government been telling us rubbish like "we're all equal" and "everyone deserves their rights" and crap like that until now we're treated worse than these sub-human races who still live in mud-huts back home and marry their sisters.

GRAMPS:

Look, shut-up or I'm not taking yer, I'm gonna change my mind. Why can't you just bloody accept the idea of each to his own and leave it at that.

WHITE MAN:

(Pointing at the news.) I can't accept that gramps because now these curry-stinking Pakis are blowing us up and trying to make our country into a Muslim harem.

GRAMPS:

Bloody hell, they ain't half taught you well at your "meetings".

WHITE MAN:

You better believe it gramps. They were giving us a detailed investigation of the Quran as well. Did you know that it tells them

Pakis to kill all non-Muslims whenever they get the chance? No wonder they're killing everyone-it tells them to in their book!

GRAMPS:

Look, don't believe everything you hear at your political meetings, right, and by the way, and I mean it, any ranting and raving while we're in the Oz and you're on the first plane back home. I'm going there for a rest, to end my life in the sun, the sand, to see me old pals and that's all- imagine you going there with all your ideas-you'll muddy the waters.

WHITE MAN:

Cross my heart and hope to die, stick a needle in my eye, I promise I won't spoil it for yer, I'll be too busy with my new found "friends'. *(Hourglass gesture.)*

GRAMPS:

(Noticing the TV.) Terrorists caught and Rossperg situation, as usual. Hey, what about these toasters speaking to people, I've never heard anything like it.

WHITE MAN:

Bloody Bible-bashing Americans, that's what it is- I bet it's another one of these publicity stunts like the so-called 'bloke' who got pregnant. Hey, hang about, they don't have many queers in the Oz do they gramps?

GRAMPS:

Each to his own son, each to his own.

WHITE MAN:

They better not have- two things I hate the most, bloody immigrants and queers- whole point I'm going is to get away from the whole bloody lot of them.

GRAMPS:

Well mind your own business and you'll be alright. By the way don't forget to pick up the stuff from up town, do you remember!

WHITE MAN:

Course I do mate, I'll drive down later on. Anyway, the toaster- I heard that this man reckons the toaster told him that judgment day is on its way. It's probably judgment day for the poor toast as well gramps, what da ya reckon eh? Two toast burned to a crisp, portents of the coming of the hour, and a shitty breakfast at the same time. *(Lights fade.)*

SCENE SEVEN

(In the lift. The three sit as before in their triangular formation, staring vacantly into their hopes and fears. The phone buzzes, the white man presses the button this time.)

SHOPPING CENTRE MANAGER'S VOICE:

Hi there, just checking in, am I right in saying that everything is okay with you guys?

WOMAN:

Yes, we're still alive.

SHOPPING CENTRE MANAGER'S VOICE:

And can I just confirm with you that you are all sitting down on each side of lift?

MUSLIM:

That would be correct- but I'm sure that when you go over all the recorded material you'll find mine and this gentleman's altercation.

SHOPPING CENTRE MANAGER'S VOICE:

I'm sure I will. And just for the record, we have only half an hour left my engineers assure me, and you will find the lift brings you up to the next level and you can be on your way.

WHITE MAN:

That will be the happiest moment of my life, bar the night I lost my virginity with a blonde, twelve-stone bit of rump (The *Muslim frowns.*) Oops, sorry Abdul!

WOMAN:

Any news about our phones?

SHOPPING CENTRE MANAGER'S VOICE:

I'm sorry, no explanation about that I'm afraid, you'll just have to wait until you are out of the lift and contact your service provider. Okay, I'll be back to you soon.

(*The woman is frowning.*)

WOMAN:

I'm sorry. I can't help but notice that you'll find any excuse to express your pathetic sense of your own masculinity. More like depravity.

WHITE MAN:

In English please sweet-heart.

MUSLIM:

The way I understand it, she's trying to say you're always trying to show off, so just give us break while we have to share the same lift in these special circumstances, we're not asking for much, just sit there quietly until the lift gets working again and we can all leave happily.

WHITE MAN:

I bet you don't even know what masculinity is, do you Abdul?

MUSLIM:

My name is not Abdul, so don't bloody patronise me by calling me that again, and for your information white boy, I know exactly what masculinity is, I've been married for four years.

WHITE MAN:

Oh yeh! Any kids?

MUSLIM:

No, *(embarrassed.)* but...

WHITE MAN:

Oh, I hope you haven't got any... problems?

MUSLIM:

What?! You are total twat of a man, aren't you? It's none of your business and I don't know why I'm discussing this with total stranger, anyway. Oh, when will this end?

WOMAN:

Don't worry, only thirty more minutes, I'm counting. (*Lights fade.*)

SCENE EIGHT

(The lights reveal the woman's apartment which is avant-garde with two gigantic photographs above the mantle, the first of the woman with her partner and the second, a copy of a classical painting of the mythical female race, The Amazons. The woman assumes the same position and situation as the men and she is counting cash.

The radical feminist woman is a successful artist who lives with her partner, Hope. Hope is an administrator and they have been together for many years. Hope does interact socially with men but the woman has now for a long time given up any social friendships with the male species and only keeps to formalities believing the male species to be too problematic and dangerous to engage with. Her hatred and bitterness towards the opposite gender are exceptional.)

(The outside door is heard unlocking and the woman's partner comes in with a bunch of flowers and shiny cardboard bags filled with presents.)

HOPE:

Hi!

WOMAN:

Hi, *(They exchange a welcoming kiss.)* How was it?

HOPE:

Aw! It was so sweet. As you can see, they didn't spare any expense on me.

WOMAN:

Oh, so they spoiled you and... Yuck! I bet the men chose those. *(Indicating the bags.)*

HOPE:

No, sorry to disappoint you this time, but this wasn't the men's doing, it was my line-manager.

WOMAN:

You don't mean the lovely, cuddly, hetro-queen.

HOPE:

Yes, the well-rounded, many delivered, mother of men did it again, before I left she managed to smother me with her big, fat lips and frankly nearly assaulted me with her swinging hips!

WOMAN:

(Laughing.) Oh, you poor thing.

HOPE:

She gave this outrageously embarrassing speech at the end. You should have heard her *(Mimicking.)* "We're saddened to see our own bit of hope, departing into the horizon, leaving us behind with a feeling of despair".

WOMAN:

Oh, that puts the "cor" back into corny I think.

HOPE:

Yeh, and here's the best bit, towards the end she wished us some luck: "I would just like to wish Hope and her partner, a woman, the best of luck in their new home and place of work"

WOMAN:

You're kidding, she actually said your partner "a woman"?

HOPE:

I'm not kidding. I think it slipped out.

WOMAN:

Slipped out! Sounds like downright discrimination to me.

HOPE:

Oh, I don't mind. But it was really funny, the rest of the department just couldn't stop laughing and ridiculing her afterwards. That woman will never be able to socialise with non-hetros; she's just too uncultured.

WOMAN:

Too fattened with the seed of men I'd say. Well, I expect you're glad to see the back of her.

HOPE:

I'll miss her in a way, especially as, where we're going to, there won't be any normal, annoying ignorant people to contend with.

WOMAN:

Do I detect another barrage of second thoughts?

HOPE:

Well, it is scary I think, just the thought of it.

WOMAN:

We've already talked about this. It's scary if you still have a trace of sympathy for a world ruled by unruly, unruleable men.

HOPE:

Yes, but we will be surrounded by large groups of females- I still can't get over the prospect of there being a great deal of arguing and fussing around.

WOMAN:

There are arguments in any community.

HOPE:

Yes, but do you not think we're chasing a dream which may not materialise. Many have tried and failed.

WOMAN:

Yes, but this is a commune with a difference. It's already a success as an autonomous community. Last time I heard they were up to 300 women living there and that the houses were ready for new people to move in. *(Pause.)* It hurts when you show doubt.

HOPE:

I just don't want to be let down, feeling there may be a community we've been looking for and instead end up in a cult. I'm not in it for a cult, I want to live with some sisters, contemplating the freshness of the land and the beauty of the landscape. That's all. Activism is for people who don't age- there can be an immaturity about it. Fighting against things which can never been vanquished by fighting.

WOMAN:

I'm not an activist, I'm a realist. Men are dangerous, incompetent and constantly afraid of their impotence, so they use their genetic physical advantages to oppress the rest of the human race. That is reality. Men commit most violent crime, men have a fixation about mounting women, and men only live to satisfy their lusts. Simple. I'm moving away to protect myself and I'm taking you with me because I want to protect the woman I love.

HOPE:

Oh! So you've become the hunter-gatherer now!

WOMAN:

Imagine that, no more men in sight.

HOPE:

Isn't the community situated in a valley?

WOMAN:

No more idiots falling about on the streets at night.

HOPE:

Surrounded by valleys instead of rows of concrete.

WOMAN:

No more fear of walking alone at night.

HOPE:

No more fear of getting run over in rush hour traffic!

WOMAN:

Oh stop your flippancy will you?

HOPE:

What?! You want to get away from the male species, and I want to get away from the enclosed spaces of this ever-shrinking world of ours. *(Goes over and puts arm around the woman.)* I'm only teasing by way. I'm looking forward to going, I can't wait, it will be really good to get away. But I'm not like you. I don't particularly hate men, but I do particularly love women.

WOMAN:

You keep your eyes yourself when we get there.

HOPE:

You know what I mean. Anyway, we just have to agree to disagree. You're going because you hate men and I'm going because I love women, let's settle with that.

WOMAN:

You'll understand one day, when the male species show you their true colours.

HOPE:

Oh, and I'm so innocent that I've never seen their true colours before? Give me some credit at least my love!

WOMAN:

Their true colours, my darling Hope, their true colours, what's hidden underneath... *(Lights fade.)*

SCENE NINE

(In the lift. The scene resumes with the Muslim, the white man and the woman. They are sitting, as before, at each side of the lift, staring out blankly.

Suddenly the lift shudders, violently. This rouses the characters, who look around apprehensively.

The white man reaches for the speaker button and presses it to alert the manager.)

WHITE MAN:

Hello! What the bloody hell is going on up there? *(There is no answer. He presses the button again.)* Hello!? Do you hear me!? Hello!

(The lift continues to shake, violently. The white man presses the speaker button desperately to gain some contact. The other two grip on to the sides in panic.

Finally, the trembling stops, the speaker seems to be working.)

WHITE MAN:

Bloody hell mate, we're being thrown about down here, what's going on? *(The speaker can be heard crackling slightly, but no-one speaks.)* Hello?

MUSLIM:

Speakers have probably cut out after the disturbance.

WHITE MAN:

No, they can't have cut out, they must be able to hear us! Oi, John whatever your bloody name is!

(The white man listens for a while, realises he's getting no answer and just sits back.)

WOMAN:

Well, now what?

WHITE MAN:

We just wait here until the cords snap and we go hurtling down to the ground at top speed. Lovely thought eh?

WOMAN:

I guess any hope for a sensible reply out of you is out of the question.

MUSLIM:

No, wait, this must be temporary. I'm sure they've realised that they can't get through to us and they'll being shouting down to us for reassurance. Just wait and see.

(They wait in silence, expecting some kind of contact from above. Many moments pass by without any sign of activity from the speakers or above.)

WHITE MAN:

Oh forget this, I'm gonna bloody get out this lift and climb up, I've had enough. *(He looks carefully at the ceiling.)*

MUSLIM:

I don't think that's a good idea mate. We should wait until they contact us.

WHITE MAN:

I'm not waiting for no man, I've had enough, they're messing us around and I'm gonna take some action of me own.

WOMAN:

How on earth will you get out of the lift?

WHITE MAN:

This ceiling must pop out or something, haven't you seen the films?

WOMAN:

Okay, so we're counting on films for our escape. Fine. Where will you go once you're out of the lift?

WHITE MAN:

I'll climb up to the next level and force the doors open and be on my way, leaving you two love birds to enjoy the last remaining minutes of your life before the lift crushes you.

MUSLIM:

And what if they get the lift working and it starts moving towards you?

WHITE MAN:

(After deliberating.) Okay, you got any other bright ideas Mr Mullah?

MUSLIM:

Yes, wait for the engineers to get us out.

WHITE MAN:

If we wait, the only way they'll be getting us out is by cutting us out.

WOMAN:

You're a very calming influence. Aren't you Mr Britain?

WHITE MAN:

No, it's called realism. Why beat about the bush? We could die here, lie or no lie?

MUSLIM:

You're beginning to sound a little bit hysterical mate, don't you think?

WHITE MAN:

(Mimicking in an Indian accent.) You're beginning to sound a little bit hysterical... Do you know how many people die a year in lift accidents? Bloody loads pal, bloody loads.

MUSLIM:

As long as we stay calm and wait we'll be okay.

WHITE MAN:

You can stay calm, I'm gonna get myself out of here. *(He begins to shout and bang on the ceiling, jumping up.)* Oi! Get us out of here!

MUSLIM:

You'll disturb the lift you idiot! Stop that! *(Moves towards the white man.)*

WHITE MAN:

Don't you frigging come near me Abdul, don't even lay one of your dirty fingers on me.

MUSLIM:

(Threateningly.) If you continue to endanger us, I'll have no choice.

WOMAN:

Look this isn't getting us anywhere!

MUSLIM:

Stop what you're doing and stand back. *(Face to face with the white man.)*

WHITE MAN:

I don't take orders from anyone, especially someone like you.

MUSLIM:

Yeh, well then I'll have to teach you otherwise.

WOMAN:

(Screaming.) Stop this now!!!

(At this moment, the lift cords are heard snapping, the lift jolts downwards. The white man desperately presses the button but there is no answer. The three start yelling for help and assistance but none comes. The lift becomes still and the three sit back down and go silent for a while.)

WHITE MAN:

(In a stupor.) I don't bloody believe this. I'm going to die, in a lift, with a Paki and a Lesbian.

WOMAN:

(Becoming increasingly fearful and paranoid.) I know what this is all about. I've figured it out. You two planned this didn't you. You all planned this, the manager, you and you, three men. You just waited until you got somebody and then you planned to trap me in the lift so that you could have your way. And the dirty man upstairs can get turned on watching you.

MUSLIM:

(Paranoia creeping in.) No, this is a one of your kuffar mind tricks, isn't it? This is your Reality TV, designed to ridicule a Muslim, deliberately place me with a bunch a stinking kafirs, a racist and a homosexual, well come out, where ever you are, come out! Show yourself? I'm on to you!

WHITE MAN:

No my friend, we've figured you out. This is one of your plans. This is one of your Muslim suicides, one of your attacks against our way of life, against our people. You and your friends have blown up the whole shopping centre and now you're going to try and kill us, I've figured you out!

(They now almost speak simultaneously, speaking with intense disgust and hatred but never giving eye contact.)

WOMAN:

You want to infect me with your diseased members because you're rotten, disgusting, scum! You'll have to kill me first before you can have your rotten way with my decomposing body, scum!

MUSLIM:

You want to infect my faith with your nasty, deviant, evil ways because you're hell-bound disbelievers! You'll have to kill me before I give in to your misguidance, do you hear me, I will never submit to you.

WHITE MAN:

You want to make everyone Muslim so you can fill the nation with your mosques and your veiled woman, you want to kill us and convert our children. Well, before you kill me, I'll kill as many of yours first.

(Suddenly, the speakers crackle to indicate they are live, a series of sounds are heard like a radio being tuned in. It is as if the speakers of the lift are picking up radio signals and broadcasting them to the occupants of the lift. The three become silent. From now on we experience the supernatural interventions of the "awakened" lift more explicitly, whereas before the interventions were subtle. We can now deduce that the lift was behind all the general mysteries, like the CCTV discrepancy and so on. A few items during this tuning sequence stand out for a while before passing into the unintelligible switching of channels, like they hear an extract from the news about Rossperg.)

VOICE OF NEWS CASTER:

In a dramatic turn of events Rossperg is facing a civil war scenario as the separatist militias have suddenly turned against each other and are now fighting against the state and themselves in the space of 24 hours.

(And we hear a comment from Rosspergan Minister, Roman Fattansis).

ROMAN FATTANSIS'S VOICE:

The dangerous ideologies of these separatists can only fragment and disintegrate our culture and identity as a civilised, progressive nation,

(And also from the suicide video from the terrorists.)

MUSHTAQ TAKFIR'S VOICE:

We're doing this because we've had enough of your world and want to make a world without you.

(We then hear the American man with the miraculous toaster.)

AMERICAN MAN'S VOICE:

I've never seen anything like it, like it was a miracle from the Lord Jesus.

WHITE MAN:

This is madness! How is this stuff getting through?

(The tuning stops. We then hear the background noise of the shopping centre with the chorus of shoppers busily walking by, and with the same nauseating music. After a while, the speakers seem to pick up the private conversations of people old and young actually in the centre at that very same moment in time. Comments heard include:)

SHOP ASSISTANT'S VOICE:

Yes, they fit you perfectly, you look wonderful. And that's what really matters madam that you look wonderful in them.

SHOPPING CENTRE MANAGER'S VOICE

Here's our little staff area that you and other Saturdays workers can use, there's tea, coffee and a fridge. Our only rule is that we don't talk about religion or politics in here

SECURITY GUARD'S VOICE:

I tell you what it's like Rossperg in here, we've got these stupid gangs of youth causing trouble again.

MEMBER OF PUBLIC'S VOICE:

Oh yes, I heard about it on the news, say there could be a civil war. People don't learn do they? Anyway, back to the real news of the hour, have you heard about what young Tracy, Grace's daughter's been up to?

SHOP ASSISTANT'S VOICE:

Can I interest you in some electrical appliances sir?

CUSTOMER'S VOICE:

Yes, just as long as they don't talk to me mate!

(They share a laugh. At this the sound stops for a moment.)

MUSLIM:

How on earth is this coming through the speakers? This has to be some kind of trick? I mean who are these voices?

WOMAN:

You heard them. It's coming from the people in the shopping centre?

MUSLIM:

Yes but how is it coming through. It must be something to do with the CCTV.

WHITE MAN:

Something is not bloody right here and I don't know what.

(Suddenly, the speakers work again, and we hear another seemingly live conversation being tuned into. The three are quiet. The Muslim becomes extremely uncomfortable and then stares out in total confusion. He can hear his wife's voice, Asia, coming through the speakers.)

ASIA'S VOICE:

How are you doing sis?

SISTER'S VOICE:

The question should be how are you doing Mrs traveller-to-be?

ASIA'S VOICE:

Yes, I'm fine, just mentally preparing myself.

WHITE MAN:

Who the bloody hell are these people and how and why is this conversation coming into the lift!?

WOMAN:

I know, yes, I've got it. It's been in the news recently about phone calls being broadcasted onto radio, well this must be a similar thing.

MUSLIM:

That's my wife's voice.

WHITE MAN:

You what?

MUSLIM:

(Blankly, confused.) That's my wife speaking to her sister. What is going here?

WOMAN:

It can't be. You're mistaken. That's just impossible, unbelievable, what are the odds of this happening?

MUSLIM:

I don't know about the odds and luck, but all I know is that's my wife talking to her sister and I don't understand what is happening here, it doesn't make any sense.

(The phone conversation continues.)

ASIA'S VOICE:

I'm happy I'm going, the package sounds great and it will be amazing living in the holy lands, we can visit the holy cities whenever we want. I've just got this nagging feeling.

SISTER'S VOICE:

That sounds ominous.

ASIA'S VOICE:

My husband isn't like he used to be when we first got together. He's changed and deep down I know I don't feel the same way anymore. He takes things so seriously.

(The Muslim sits confused, dejected. Before anyone else can comment another conversation comes through the speakers rousing the three people.)

GRAMP'S VOICE:

So Charlie, I'll be with you very soon.

CHARLIE'S VOICE:

Be looking forward to seeing yer mate!

GRAMP'S VOICE:

Just wanted to tell yer though, I'm bringing me grandson with me.

CHARLIE'S VOICE:

You mean the British bulldog himself!

GRAMPS' VOICE:

Afraid so. He don't half talk a load of crap let me tell you. Anyway, as long as he minds his own business I'll be alright. Promised his mam I'd look after him, and I tell you what, if she hadn't asked me to I would have been better off without him. You should see the way he's turned out. A bum, a big lousy good for nothing bum who blames everyone but himself! But I do have a little soft spot for him, seeing as he's my little girl's wee nipper. Can you line him up with some work?

(The white man has been quiet throughout and has withdrawn into a stupor. Another conversation filters through the feedback. The woman shrinks back.)

HOPE'S VOICE:

Yes we're finally going. But I don't know. She's just so anti-men it's becoming a joke. I mean, you'd understand if she had some kind of history. But she hasn't and I don't understand where she's got all this hatred from. She does irritate me sometimes, and I'm worried a bit about isolating myself from the rest of the world in an all-female kind of Utopia. She doesn't realise that I do actually get on with a few men rather well.

(The conversation finishes. The speakers go silent. The characters stare out in shock.)

(Suddenly, the lift's phone starts buzzing, the woman involuntarily moves and presses the speaker button. The unearthly and distant voice of the lift speaks)

THE LIFT:

I am Lift, request your direction

(Time stops. The woman almost in a trance moves forward.)

WOMAN:

I want to live with women only.

THE LIFT:

Why?

WOMAN:

(Revealing her inner feelings,) I just want to live in a place where I can feel safe and comfortable. I don't feel safe around men. They scare me. I see all these gangs of young men roaming around and I think to myself that they have lost control. In fact, they seem to be unable to stop themselves, as if their wildness is part of their instincts. I want to be away from them. That's all. Can't you understand? I just want to be at peace and live with people who give me peace. I can't feel peace where I am now. Don't I sound reasonable to you? I don't want to hurt anyone, deep down I intend no harm towards anyone. I just want to live in happiness with my own kind. Take me to a place of women.

THE LIFT:

I will take you in that direction.

(The lift moves downwards and then stops. The doors are heard opening.)

THE LIFT:

Level 3. Women Only.

(The woman walks out of the lift. The Muslim and the white man remain).

(The phone rings as before. The two men remain seated in a stupor, totally oblivious of the fact that the woman has left the lift. The white man presses the button activating the speaker, as if he is almost in hypnosis.)

THE LIFT:

I am lift. I can send you in the opposite direction, what is your request?

WHITE MAN:

A place for the white race.

THE LIFT:

Why?

WHITE MAN:

I can't mix with foreigners and I never will. They have spoiled and changed my way of life. There's still a chance to get our way back, but we have to be brave- we have to remain pure. Now if it means live and let live, that's fine. But not together. Live separate and let live separate. That's the way, that's what I ask for. Let the others live in their way and I'll live with my own people our way. Do you understand? I won't harm anyone, I won't take anyone's land, I won't civilise, I'll just let them be. All I want is a place that I can call home and people who I can say are really my people. Does that sound unreasonable to you? That's all I want. Send me to the place of the white race.

THE LIFT:

I will take you in that direction.

(The lift begins to move downwards and then stops.)

THE LIFT

Level 2: The Master Race. (The white man walks out of the lift leaving only the Muslim).

(The speaker phone rings. In a trance, the Muslim answers the ringing phone, the lift speaks as before.)

THE LIFT:

I am lift. I can send you in the opposite direction, what is your request.

MUSLIM:

To live with the saved sect.

VOICE OF THE LIFT:

Why?

MUSLIM:

I don't just want to be away from those who don't believe. I want to away from the misguidance of those who claim to believe. They are the cancer from within and the kaffirs are the cancer from outside. I want to keep my self, my thoughts and my heart purified of disbelief, of misguidance, and erroneous ideas and innovations. I want to live in a state of purity, with the people of purity. That's all I ask for. Don't you want to be rid of me and my kind? Wouldn't you be happy to rid yourselves of all of us? You can all live together in your deluded happiness, and we can live away from you, everyone is happy. Why do you insist that we have to live together?

THE LIFT:

I will take you in that direction.

(The Lift move downwards then stops. The doors are heard opening.)

THE LIFT:

Level 1- The Saved Sect.

(The lift remains empty; the ding-dong goes on and off and the lift announces like a computer malfunctioning.)

THE LIFT:

I am lift, I am idle and I wait for your request *(Repeatedly, rising in tension and intensity). (Lights fade.)*

SCENE TEN

(In the shopping centre manager's office. The manager sits at his desk looking at four different CCTV screens. Also, in the room is the assistant manager looking on.)

SHOPPING CENTRE MANAGER:

(using his walkie-talkie, talking to engineer.) The camera in the lift has gone off, as has the phone/speaker system. What's going on, over?

ENGINEER'S VOICE:

Nothing do to with me. Check your systems, it's probably temporary. I've heard of disturbances around the area. I'm nearly finished here. Over.

SHOPPING CENTRE MANAGER:

Okay, keep me informed, over and out.

ENGINEER'S VOICE:

Roger that! Over and out.

SHOPPING CENTRE MANAGER:

Well, our fellows in the lift will just have to wait for a while until the lift gets going. You don't think they're killing each other do you?

ASSISTANT MANAGER:

(Laughing.) I tell you what, that woman sounded like she was in her worst nightmare! Stuck between a Muslim and a yob! Poor thing.

SHOPPING CENTRE:

No, no we shouldn't be so flippant about the whole thing. Why, at this very moment they're probably having a most civilised chat.

ASSISTANT MANAGER:

Or the Muslim has converted them all to Islam, or the skin-head has probably nutted both of them, or possibly the woman has convinced them to have a sex change! Did you hear her earlier on: 'Your deluded sense of your own masculinity.'

SHOPPING CENTRE MANAGER:

We still have some footage of them. I reckon you could sell it to a reality TV show or post it on social media. The day three weirdos got stuck together in a lift and the resulting mayhem. It would make compulsive viewing. We could make millions, become famous.

ASSISTANT MANAGER:

Actually, it would make perfect material for a Nature programme. Observing survival instincts within three endangered species.

SHOPPING CENTRE MANAGER:

I don't know about endangered. Seem to be a lot of weirdos popping up everywhere these days.

ASSISTANT MANAGER:

Speaking of weirdos, I was watching this programme about this cult in the US who moved away from the city and founded their own little society. Turns out the founder was considered like a prophet, and when his prediction for judgement day didn't come true, they all went and killed themselves. And get this. They never found his body. Their prophet never went through with it! I mean how twisted is that? And how stupid were the rest!

SHOPPING CENTRE MANAGER:

I tell you what mate, I'm not surprised by that.

ASSISTANT MANAGER:

And guess what else. Now this is probably the most chilling part. They all recorded suicide messages. One of them said he'd moved away from the hell of the modern world and had found heaven in his new place. Then he said that something was calling for him to join his brethren in that place in the sky. Then the wacko and all his mates injected themselves and their children with doses of cyanide. Lovely thought eh?

SHOPPING CENTRE MANAGER:

People like that should be made into eunuchs before they can go forth and multiply.

ASSISTANT MANAGER:

Yeh, and then maybe deposited onto another planet. Rights how's our engineer doing then?

(*Lights Fade.*)

SCENE ELEVEN

(We are back with the lift. The lift is empty. After silence, the lift resumes its programme.)

THE LIFT

(Announces.) Level 1.

(The Muslim walks onto the lift- stunned. The lift moves on, stops and announces.)

THE LIFT:

Level 2

(The white man walks on to the other side of the Muslim with an expression of weathered anguish, the lift continues, announces.)

THE LIFT:

Level 3

(The woman comes on and stands in the middle, humbled. The lift remains stationery. The three characters remain still.)

THE LIFT:

(To the Muslim.) What of your destination?

MUSLIM:

(Distracted.) I found myself in paradise,

with fountains, angels and fruit,

I saw a rainbow of people

Who were drinking from a brook,

They were the special people

They were the chosen ones,

But before I could unite with them

I saw an envious devil,

A wicked, odious thing,

Bitter and malignant

Who hated all but me,

Something echoed in my soul,

This devil haunted me,

I looked into its crooked face,

And recognised my identity

(The Muslim withdraws.)

THE LIFT

(To the white man.) What of your destination?

WHITE MAN:

I saw the master race,

The purest pedigree

I saw a world of white people

Who cradled and comforted me,

For miles and miles I looked ahead,

All my people shone so pure,

Their skin, their ways, their families

I felt proud to be of them.

But just before they accepted me

Something hung to my leg,

It was a dirty darkie,

Who looked at all with pride,

I looked into his lecherous face,

And saw my jealous eye.

(The white man withdraws.)

THE LIFT

(To the woman.) What of your destination?

WOMAN:

I saw a sea of sisterhood,

Naked and interlinked,

I let myself fall in

And felt their hearts beating.

My sisters shored me up with love,

My lovers cradled me,

The deeper that I plummeted

My sisters were my strength.

But then I reached the inner core,

I found an aching womb,

Inside there grew a bitter man,

Whose face was as my own

(All three stand, dumbfounded.)

THE LIFT:

(To the Muslim.) Do you require to travel in the same direction?

(The Muslim gives an excuse, pained, frustrated, trapped.)

MUSLIM:

Are you trying to put me down you stinkin kafir? This another one your silly stunts? I am better than you, and I do not fear you, I only fear my lord. Did you hear that stinkin, dirty kuff? The lord, Allah, the one, the Almighty, the Powerful. You are nothing, you will not be worth a bead of the sweat dripping down a donkey's arse on the judgement day. I fear you not. I'm not the one who is running, it's you. *(pause)* I'm not running from anyone, I can face myself, I can face death you dirty kuff, can you? No, you don't like to be alone, you don't like to think about death, coz you love this stinkin world of yours you kafir! I'm not afraid of dying, I know what's coming next, and I'm gonna enjoy seeing your face burned to ashes and then burned and burned and burned again. So I know where I'm going, don't you ask me where I'm going. *(He retreats.)*

THE LIFT:

(To the white man.) Do you require to travel in the same direction?

WHITE MAN:

(Like the Muslim, pacing up and down.) You stupid Pakis think you've got one up on us don't yer, bloody trapped me and think

your gonna pound the hell outta me, and shall I tell you what? You ain't got the guts to take me one on one because you're a bunch of Paki cowards aren't yer? You bloody live in your little mud huts in Pakiland, then you come here and take our stuff, and when we come and try and get it back, you gather in a little orgi and try to beat us off, you bunch of brown pussies. You are parasites, you're not good enough to live with us, so why do you bother us? Wherever you go you have to pitch up your little mud huts don't yer? And you bring your mosques and halal meat, and then you think you're equal to us, but you're not- you can't admit that we're better than you are, so don't you bloody tell me where to go you stupid parasite, you can't tell me where to go. *(He retreats.)*

THE LIFT:

(To the women.) Do you require to travel in the same direction?

WOMAN:

Scum, scum, scum, scum. I smell the sweat and the fear of a piece of scum. You're sweating because I dare to defy you, I won't listen to you, I want to be rid of you, I don't need you. You're sweating because I'm cutting the cord and then I'm threatening to twist it around your neck and head and squeeze until you burst scum. Are you listening scum? You're afraid because I'm giving birth without you, because I'm making love without you- because you can't survive without me scum, can you? You'll just rot away in your own muck if I wasn't there for you scum. You'd just wither away for the pathetic, waste of organic matter that you are. I can make my own way, scum, I don't need you to ask me where I'm going, I not telling you where I'm going.

THE LIFT

If you continue travelling in the same direction you will stop and become idle.

MUSLIM:

I am saved and all others are in the fire.

THE LIFT:

If you continue travelling in the same direction you will stop and become idle.

WHITE MAN:

I am the master race, and ethnics are disease.

THE LIFT:

If you continue travelling in the same direction you will stop and become idle.

WOMAN:

I will live and prosper and all scum will decompose.

THE LIFT:

(Rings out, growing in volume and intensity.) STOP AND BECOME IDLE, STOP AND BECOME IDLE, STOP AND BECOME IDLE, STOP AND BECOME IDLE STOP AND BECOME IDLE STOP AND BECOME IDLE STOP AND BECOME IDLE STOP AND BECOME IDLE *(The characters cover their ears and writhe in pain.)*

(At this moment the shopping centre manager and engineer cheer because they have got the lift working.)

THE LIFT:

(Stops screaming and suddenly announces.) I have a request in the opposite direction.

(The characters wake up as if recovering from a nightmare, standing, disorientated.)

WOMAN:

How long have we been here?

MUSLIM:

It seems like hours?

WHITE MAN:

Did we fall asleep?

MUSLIM:

No, we've just been sitting here, probably dozed off.

(They look at the phone gingerly. It begins to ring. They freeze, almost reminded by some terrible menace they have recently been exposed to. The Muslim edges to the phone and presses the speaker button. To their relief, it is the Shopping Centre Manager.)

SHOPPING CENTRE MANAGER'S VOICE:

Great new guys, the engineer has just about cracked the problem and you should be out in the next few minutes.

WOMAN:

How long have we been here for?

SHOPPING CENTRE MANAGER'S VOICE:

What? Has it been that much of a trauma for you, really sorry for the inconvenience, you've been there for about an hour. By the way, sorry about the loss of speaker coverage, we had some kind of technical failure. The CCTV cameras blanked out in the whole centre for a few minutes. As did the music system. Very strange! Anyhow you'll be out very soon, I promise!

MUSLIM:

I think we may have fallen asleep.

SHOPPING CENTRE MANAGER

Yes, you seemed all to be wrapped up in your own thoughts for a while there. Must be boring stuck in a boring lift. Never mind, you'll be out in a tick. Music will be back on soon as well. Do you have any requests?

(They freeze.)

WHITE MAN:

No. Thank you.

SHOPPING CENTRE MANAGER'S VOICE:

Okay, I'll get the music going again for you.

(The nauseating music begins again. The three people stand in an indescribable awkwardness. They are struck between giving in to the aching realisation that the past events really happened or that they had hallucinated the whole thing.)

WOMAN:

Something isn't right.

WHITE MAN:

What do you mean?

WOMAN:

Something's not right, something's happened?

MUSLIM:

What are you talking about?

WOMAN:

While we were asleep.

WHITE MAN:

We weren't asleep, we were just standing here.

WOMAN:

No we weren't.

WHITE MAN:

Look sweetheart, we have been stuck in this place for so long that we're getting frustrated, so just cool it and we'll be out soon.

WOMAN:

Don't you feel it?

WHITE MAN:

O my god, she's gonna say we did something to her.

MUSLIM:

I feel like I want to be out of here and go home.

WOMAN:

Don't you remember? We heard those conversations.

WHITE MAN:

Which conversations? What are you talking about?

WOMAN:

We heard people we know on the phone, in this lift.

WHITE MAN:

Now you really are losing a grip on reality.

WOMAN:

Don't bloody patronise me. You know exactly what I'm talking about. We heard what our loved one really thought of us. You heard your wife speaking to her sister. And you heard some old man. There's some reason behind this. We were supposed to hear that.

MUSLIM:

I don't believe it. My wife loves me, I know my wife. That wasn't my wife.

WOMAN:

Oh, come on! Don't you remember that voice?

WHITE MAN:

Which voice?

WOMAN:

On the phone? It was the lift.

WHITE MAN:

Oh, now you heard the lift speaking to you. Have a look in her bag and you'll find her medication no doubt.

WOMAN:

I didn't just hear it, you two heard it too.

WHITE MAN:

Oh, so now you're not the only insane person, but you're including us with you. Listen, Miss Greer, don't bloody play around with us, because we don't bloody want to know alright. I tell you what Abdul, but we might be in, correction, you might be in for some bother, when we get back up and she starts talking about you trying to blow us all up or something.

MUSLIM:

That's not funny you stupid twat, you're out of order.

WHITE MAN:

Just warning yer pal, before they take you away, try and put some sense into her and we'll all have a peaceful way home.

MUSLIM:

I think you should be more worried mate.

WHITE MAN:

About what?

(They begin to square up to each other. As the intimidation intensifies, the woman has been showing a sickly expression, and looks like she is about to vomit, and suddenly, instead of vomiting she expresses.)

WOMAN:

STOP AND BECOME IDLE? STOP AND BECOME IDLE STOP AND BECOME IDLE STOP AND BECOME IDLE?!

(They all freeze, then sit down and stare out as they did before. The lift starts working and moves upwards. The three are silent and thoughtful while the lift goes up. Just before the lift reaches its destination, the speaker emits a muddled collection of quotes from the people involved and the lift.)

THE LIFT:

Travelling in the same direction

VOICE OF WHITE MAN:

We're not treated the way we used to be.

THE LIFT:

Remaining in that same direction

VOICE OF THE MUSLIM:

You'll see these people for what they really are.

THE LIFT:

If there are no further changes

VOICE OF THE WOMAN:

I don't find any peace

THE LIFT:

If there are no further requests

VOICE OF ROMAN FATTANSIS:

Can only fragment our culture and identity,

THE LIFT:

Or stop and become idle

VOICE OF HOPE:

We only hate what lives in ourselves

THE LIFT:

I can only follow your requests, or stop and become idle.

I can only follow your requests, or stop and become idle,

I can only follow your requests, or stop and become idle.

(The lift comes to a halt and announces, Level 1 Car Park and Exit. The individuals leave without saying a word. Lights fade.)

SCENE TWELVE

(The newscaster from before appears again with the final newscast of the day.)

NEWS ANCHORMAN:

Hello and tonight's top stories.

In another amazing development, separatist militias in Rossperg have called a ceasefire to their recent in-fighting and conflict, while the Rosspergan authorities have remained silent about whether they will continue military strikes. Rosspergan officials are expected to hold a press-conference later on today where we will provide live coverage. Roman Fattansis said earlier today, and I quote him here: "This crisis threatens to de-stabilise the very foundations of our world. We must not let these terrorists change the direction we are going in, which is the direction of human progress and enlightenment. We must all live together as one under the rules and laws we have all-chosen to adhere to. This separatism is just a sign of barbarism and must be stopped. But we are still discussing our next moves".

And a leader of the militias was quoted today to have said: "Rossperg must learn that we the people of the outlying lands no longer wish to live under its jurisdiction, and we will continue to fight until our way of life is respected and given an opportunity to flourish."

More on this story later.

Once again stories of the awakening phenomenon flood the public and the government has created a research group to study what they are labelling "mass hysteria and paranoia, similar to what was witnessed in West Virginia in Point Pleasant during the 'mothman' incident, but on a wider scale". However, the public have their own views, and many religious spokespeople are beginning to prepare their flock for the coming of judgement and the fulfilment of their prophecies. The latest awakenings seem to be affecting lifts and elevators, and we have several witnesses attesting to hearing voices from lift speakers proclaiming: "Change direction or stop and become idle".

(Lights fade. Curtains.)

ABOUT THE AUTHOR

Novid Shaid is an English teacher from the UK, who has taught in various secondary schools for over seventeen years. His first published work is the mystical thriller novel: The Hidden Ones, which is available on Amazon.

He also shares short stories and poems on his website, www.novid.co.uk and can be contacted on the following email: novid@hotmail.com

www.ingramcontent.com/pod-product-compliance
Lightning Source LLC
Chambersburg PA
CBHW032113040426
42337CB00040B/405